Natalia is a young upcoming artist, who was born in Poland but currently resides in Spain. Her poems may have a tendency of outlining big feelings through even bigger metaphors. Meeting people is a difficult task (even for the most outgoing individuals) because they even have specific characteristics that they look out for when deciding whether a new stranger will be their friend. Natalia in her poems found this friend, she found herself. Although this might sound cheesy, like the starting words of a coming-of-age movie, poetry helped her be honest with herself, which is why she believes that her new book *Does the Sun Always Come Out after the Storm?* will help people have their coming-of-age moment by being honest with themselves.

For the people who helped me gain experience, without you, this book wouldn't be made.

Natalia Walczak

DOES THE SUN ALWAYS COME OUT AFTER THE STORM?

AUSTIN MACAULEY PUBLISHERS™
LONDON · CAMBRIDGE · NEW YORK · SHARJAH

Copyright © Natalia Walczak 2024

The right of Natalia Walczak to be identified as author of this work has been asserted by the author in accordance with sections 77 and 78 of the Copyright, Designs and Patents Act 1988.

All rights reserved. No part of this publication may be reproduced, stored in a retrieval system, or transmitted in any form or by any means, electronic, mechanical, photocopying, recording, or otherwise, without the prior permission of the publishers.

Any person who commits any unauthorised act in relation to this publication may be liable to criminal prosecution and civil claims for damages.

A CIP catalogue record for this title is available from the British Library.

ISBN 9781035848089 (Paperback)
ISBN 9781035848096 (ePub e-book)

www.austinmacauley.com

First Published 2024
Austin Macauley Publishers Ltd®
1 Canada Square
Canary Wharf
London
E14 5AA

First of all, I would like to thank Austin Macauley Publishers for guiding me through this journey of publishing my first book and for seeing my potential. I would also like to thank my family who were there for me not only for the production process but many times before, helping me find the sun during the storm.

Table of Contents

Storm	**11**
Self-Sabotaging	13
The Spinning Ball	14
Me and Myself	15
Failure	16
Between Black and White	17
Therapy	18
Taboo	19
Where Am I going?	20
Like on a Rollercoaster	22
Places We've Known	23
Social Experiment	24
The Unofficial Guide of the Education System	25
Final Decrees	26
Authority	27
Scorn	28
Conscious Breathing	29
Compulsion	30
Concealed	31
Habits	32
Sincere	33

Vicious Circle	34
Is That Love?	36
Do My Looks Define Me	37
Tumble	38
A Letter to a Dear Friend	39
I Feel Like I Lost Myself	40
Prison for My Thoughts	41
Home	42
Defence	43
Metal Hearts	44
Calendar Mark	45
Memoria Damnum	46
Anguish	47
Ghosts of the Past	48
Leftovers	49
Earth problems	50
Social Battery	51
Sandcastles	52
Sun	**53**
Visage	55
Somnia (Dreams)	56
Volets Bleus (Blue Shutters)	57
Time	58
Spectrum of Love	59

Storm

Self-Sabotaging

If I could go into the fire I would;
But that's too easy.
So, I suffer from the smallest things in life;
That's what brings me joy.
The more I suffer, the more I cry;
the more alive I feel later.
But what if, after some time, I won't?

I am cold, I take off my jacket.
I am warm, I put my jacket back on.
I am hungry, I throw all of the food away.
I eat too much, I prepare myself another meal.

They say, keep your enemies close;
But in this case, I wish I wouldn't.

Because to make my enemy disappear,
My whole facade would have to disappear as well.
Since my worst enemy is myself.

My brain creates problems
that some people would only dream of causing.
The things that I love, I turn into my leverage,
So that in the most vulnerable moment,
I can shoot them like bullets
Into the places that hurt the most.
Cause no one else knows what hurts the most,
Than the person that is experiencing the pain.
Eventually, my mission will be complete,
and they will all know its name.

The games will become more and more extreme;
Unless some other force stops them in time.
But if not, everyone will know the name of this mission;
The mission of sabotage.

The Spinning Ball

My mouth is sealed;
My heart is not healed.
My mind is wondering,
Along with my pride sundering.
I cannot keep the pace
Of the round ball spinning.
As I stare blankly at the wall thinking,
Thinking about the future,
But more the past.
The things worth lasting,
But quickly passing;
The things of my fault,
But quite not entirely,
While the faces of those involved, look at me frailly.
Now my body is not filled with joy,
Rather mourning a great loss:
Loss of happiness, loss of appreciation, lost with frustration.
I cannot help but to think of the time where I didn't mind
The people surrounding me at all times,
Thinking the world is nothing but kind.
Now I see through the pink glasses,
That were previously distracting my vision,
From the purpose of my existence,
from my chores and being persistent.
I wait for the time where my words would not have to rhyme
To make my soul feel better;
I wait for the days that will be filled with chatter.
I wish for "one of those days" to keep its true meaning,
But for now, I stare at the ball spinning.

Me and Myself

Me and myself are different people;
Me, is the bully; myself is the victim.
Me makes myself cry,
Me makes myself feel worthless.
Me makes myself feel confident,
Yet looks in the mirror and feels disappointed.

Me is the villain.

Myself lacks the self-esteem to even speak up,
Myself wasn't only broken by me;
Myself is the bodyguard of me,
Takes all the bad from the world and stores it.
Yet when me finds out about the stored negativity,
It fills the room with it,
Making myself even more self-conscious.

I wish me and myself would get along, and work as a team,
But such a duo would be too powerful to work out.
This is why me and myself are enemies,
killing each other every day.

Failure

Many say that failure is a part of life;
Without it, we wouldn't appreciate success.
But for me, failure limits my success,
It brings me down,
It makes me feel weak,
Makes me question my life.
It doesn't make me stronger.

When I meet with failure,
I feel hopeless and alone.
Why is failure a part of life?
Why would anyone want people to experience that sort of pain?
If that pain is considered a social norm,
What can we say about our life overall? Is it that important?
Should we cherish it?
If in reality, we cherish pain and disappointment…
Failure makes me disgusted with myself.

I can't look at myself because,
The only features I see,
are the once that I am most ashamed of.
How can one be a victim of failure and still be strong and confident?
Maybe people that are strong and confident didn't actually meet with failure?
Because if they did, either way they didn't fail because they overcame it.
However, me? I can't overcome anything.
I am even failing at being a failure…

Between Black and White

Why do things always have to be either black or white?
Why can't they be grey?
I sit on my bathroom floor;
The water traveling through my body.

I hide.
I hide from my feelings,
I hide from people.
I am tired, I am hopeless,
Eventually I look into the mirror, and I laugh so hard,
I cry.

I walk out of the misery for a while, as I leave the bathroom.
I am free, happy, pretty.
Dancing as if no one's watching.
I play, I shine.

Then, I see the bathroom doors again.
I take one-step forward and suddenly I feel blue.
I focus my eyes on one little dot on the floor,
Tears start streaming down my face.
Why is it like that? Why can't I be grey?

Therapy

My trembling chest moves up and down;
This should spare me enough air.
Why doesn't it?
I inhale.

I feel the pain of thousands of troops,
Marching through my chest.

Should I be stressed?
"How do you feel?"
Asks my therapist.

How do I feel?
I know how I feel;
The problems is, that I need a shield.

"How do you feel?"
I feel trapped,
Not by this uncomfortable feeling
Of a panic attack,
But by these questions.

So obvious, so plain.

"How do you feel?"
I need to leave.
"How about your parents?"
"How do they feel?"
I say with a grin.

Taboo

I look into your eyes;
I know you love all parts of me.
But what if you don't know all of them,
Would you still love me then?

I feel the urge to let you know me better,
But what if that matters?
For our bond,
For our future
What if the real me isn't what you expected?
Will I become neglected?

You tell me you'll love me no matter what,
But what if this "what" is greater than love?
Where acceptance isn't placed above
Any perspectives or worries,
What if you won't want me?

Where Am I going?

Where am I going?
I ask myself as I wake up,
Looking at my school bag and dishes
from yesterday's so-called 'failure'.

How many days of waking up
Will I have to label as 'failure'?
I focus my tired eyes on my reflection and see nothing.

Yet this nothing feels like everything I have.

Where am I going?
I ask myself, sitting on this all-too-uncomfortable chair,
Staring at the dancing numbers
On the front page of my notebook.

I look over to this girl,
She's smiling.
I wonder where she is going,
I'd like to follow her path,
But does she know where she is going?

Is she following someone else's path?
Or is she, like me, uncertain of her destiny?

Where am I going?
Define success, failure, happiness, sadness.
Such questions should feature in my morning test,
Yet, I see 'genetically modified organisms'
As the headline of the page,
Urging me to pour my knowledge, to define my worth.
Where am I going?
I look over to the boy that has already allowed the page to define his worth,

He seems proud.
Does he know where he is going?
Do I bother him or is he unbothered about my existence?
Does he know that I want to know where he is going?
Does he want to know where I am going?

So many questions, yet the only answer I know is uncertainty.
I feel happy, yet sad.
I feel angry, yet calm.
I know those are oxymorons,
but in my head they are repetitions.
I feel the same no matter how I define my state.
Should I cry? Should I laugh?
I have everything, but I feel like I have nothing.
I have nothing, but I feel like I have everything.

My head hurts.

A girl is dancing, to the rhythm of the song of an unknown language.
"Good job!" praises the teacher.
But how can you define whether she did a good job at expressing herself?
Isn't dance exactly that? Well then, why am I not good at it? Or am I?
Did the oldest person alive find out where they are going?
Sometimes I find myself losing the strength to find myself.

Am I selfish? Self-loving? Dramatic? Mentally ill?
Are they all the same thing?

Am I ever going to find someone friendly on the way to finding where I am going?
Or am I only destined to find myself?
Did I let myself down or let myself rise?
Am I smart or lazy? Perhaps both…

I don't think I will ever know where I am going,
And that's how I am going to get lost…

Like on a Rollercoaster

Sometimes life feels like a rollercoaster.
When you are already on the ground,
It suddenly catches you by surprise
and brings you back into the sky
Giving you no control
Over when you are going to come back
Or even if you'll survive while in the sky.
You can scream, cry, or laugh,
But while you're in the sky, no one can hear you;
No one will help you.
Instead, they stay on the ground watching you,
Laughing because they are in control,
And you are not.
Just as your hair is pulled back,
you can feel the wind on your skin.
You convince yourself that you are, in fact, okay,
But just as you do,
You feel your stomach doing backflips.
As you come crushing to the ground,
And you realise that you were, in fact, not okay…

Places We've Known

Sometimes I come back to the places that we've known but now they don't feel familiar.
It feels as if I'm an imposter
in a place full of happiness and a good atmosphere.
This place grips my throat, as if its duty is to kill the imposter,
But what they don't know is once I was one of them.
I completed the picture.
Now I am a red dot of paint that ruins the colourful canvas.
No matter what I do, a red shadow will stay over my name.
I desperately try to fit in, act as if I belong,
But without you it's not the same…

Social Experiment

Sometimes I feel like some secret agent designed me with the most, pathetic, weak and anti-survival instincts he could find and threw in:
Being smart, occasionally happy, hopeless romantic, and a person with a lot of potential,
He mixed it all together to form a mass of hell, also known as my character.
He then proceeded to put me into the natural habitat of this so-called "civilisation,"
Then settled to lead an undercover investigation into how long I will survive.
Because what else could make me so messed up?

The Unofficial Guide of the Education System

The educational system failed me
Limiting my own thoughts,
but asking me to interpret someone else's.
Teaching us how to be motivated, but taking our motivation away in a couple minutes.
Asking us to be "not like others," followed by the famous quote, "If he jumped, would you?"
Yet expecting us to follow a mark scheme
For an "in your opinion" question
That was passed down from generations to generations.

Expecting us to follow our own path, but do it exactly as everyone else.
Making us bitter, but then surprised when we don't smile.

I would jump, if I knew that it would let me follow my hopes and dreams,
Or if it was my dear friend jumping and jumping would mean I'd be with them forever,
Or if jumping made them survive,
Or if after the jump there was a trampoline that would bounce me right back.
Because there are different perspectives in life than only yours, dear teachers,
And the school system should embrace them.
So yes, the school system failed me.

Final Decrees

When you study too hard, you are seen as the obnoxious part of society.

When you study enough, you become the society.
When you study too little, you are society's downfall.
When you eat too much, you don't fit societal norms.

When you eat enough, you're not following the right diet.

When you eat too little, you don't love yourself.
When you love yourself, you're obnoxious.
When you're obnoxious, you study too hard.

When you study too hard, you eat too much,
When you eat too much, you don't fit societal norms.
When you don't fit societal norms, you are the society's downfall.
(stanza above has been repeated)
The truth is, no matter what you do, you'll be different.
Life is cruel, and there's no room for people thinking outside the box.
There is no preparation for how to deal with
Abandonment, jealousy, pity, loneliness, stress, uniqueness, or self-love.
We're programmed to follow a scheme that will eventually lead us to failure.
Normally, this fear passes, but I'm beginning to worry if mine ever will.

Authority

I am trapped,
But
Not within four grey walls painting my image as a villain.
Not in a small space, under the might of a padlock,
Or inside a chaos of waves that block,
My view of the skyline,
As the horizon blends with the great portion of water.
It's in my mind.
My mind fills itself with darkness, so deep even bats cannot see within.
There is no tape over my mouth,
No rope wrapped around my hands
Yet I have no control
Over my soul.
There is no end to this show

Scorn

I am beginning to think that my body has run out of mitochondria,
Yet, I don't know how.
But I do know the stages of transportation of blood to and away from the heart.
I know more than fifteen poems and extracts, and their meanings,
Followed by their structures and language devices that could engage the reader.
I know why people create businesses and why they fail.
I know how to get rid of a surd, or how to draw to scale.

What I don't know is how to get rid of these dark feelings,
as they do not require any dealing
With adding or subtracting.
I don't know how to inverse the situation to be happy,
And my points to be more snappy.
Why am I this unhappy?
Why can't I be more motivated?
Perhaps I am being hated
By the Universe or the Givers
Of the qualities so hard to grasp,
Even to believers.
But I do know the names of all the rivers.

Conscious Breathing

In a cage with thousands of thoughts,
Breathing in, breathing out,
But no results.
Tears streaming down my cheek,
Yet my face stays the same,
No sadness, no anger, no nothing.
Yet within me, there is commotion.
Like a tornado,
Swirling in my stomach,
Thoughts that don't let me sleep,
Robbing me of peace.
The rivers uniting, forming a big drought.
Yet I cannot shout.
They are coming and destroying everything,
Yet I let them move me from one side to another,
Like a boat adrift,
Further into the darkness between the waves,
Not letting me breathe, longing to be saved.
Thinking of the sea,
That usually made me calm.
I look down at my shaking palms,
Hoping to stop them but nothing seems to work.
Until I wrote this flow,
Words so hard to grasp in my mind,
Yet easy to outline.

Compulsion

I'm addicted to love,
I need it at all times.
When it's not there, I feel like I'm falling behind.
I need fireworks coursing in my veins,
I need someone who'd chase any trains,
That has me looking out the glass wall,
Smiling, waving, waiting until I fall,
Again into their arms.

The spiral of words
Making my heart full,
And helping me make a barrier for words that are cruel.
All that I would love to have,
But only when I'm upset,
When I need some comfort,
Yet as soon as, I come back from my emotional spirals,
And wake up my morals,
I know that love isn't for me,
Yet, my mind is sometimes hurt, and likes to dream.

Concealed

I could scream;
He wouldn't see.
I could cry;
He wouldn't hear.
I could be dying;
He wouldn't care

One part of me has wondered,
Why does he not care?
How can he just not care?
When will he care?
Does he see me as nothing?
Is his world different from mine?
Why does he not care?

Am I not a concern to him?
Am I too much of a worry?
Is it I? Who he doesn't care about?
Or that he just doesn't care?
Am I important? Am I worth it?
Would you waste your time on me?
Would you hug me if you saw tears streaming down my face?
Would you watch me fight myself
and forget what you just saw?
What would you do?

Am I nothing to him?
If I am nothing to him should he be nothing to me?
Well, why is it not like that then?

Why do I still find comfort in his arms
If they don't want to comfort me?
Why do I still find happiness in the words that he says,
when they aren't words of empathy?
Why do I still love him if his love for me is not constant?

Habits

I feel as if I'm slowly running out of my happiness,
Steadily going down the hole of hopelessness.
Though I've been in this place before,
It will never feel like home.
I let the old habits roll in,
Knowing what's about to begin.
I promised myself I wouldn't do this,
Yet now, my mind acts as if in amiss,
As if this caught her by surprise.
I feel the water in my eyes,
Should I give in?
Should I let go?
Or should I pretend that nothing is wrong?
Should I stir this pot of potions
With songs that part the oceans,
That grab my emotions all together,
And put them in a blender.
Should I convince myself it's just a phase,
Or admit it's an addiction that just cannot go away.

Sincere

I thought we had something,
That wasn't easy to break

I thought we had in common,
All the things we hate.

I am looking at the screen;
You're not the last I called.

I am questioning myself,
Though it's not my fault.

All the things you said,
I guess they weren't true

I thought I had a friend
I guess it's nothing new.

Vicious Circle

I go to school.
I come from school.
I eat my breakfast.
I eat my lunch.
I study.
And then I do it all over again.

The feeling of a vicious circle,
Where every day turns into forever.
The stress that I have,
The amount of energy that I put into life,
Takes some of it from me.

I feel like tomorrow I will be happy!
But I won't.
I feel like tomorrow will be better!
But it isn't.

The only thing that keeps me going,
Is music,
That melody through my ears that creates colourful,
But also painful memories, suddenly takes me to a world of hope.
Ironically, riding a rollercoaster makes me feel safer.
I keep missing,
The time when I felt safe everywhere,
Where life was like a breeze of fresh air.

I wish I could live:
With no goals to achieve but a life to live,
With no trouble to survive but a life where you can thrive,
Where love is easy and from talking to someone,
you don't feel dizzy.
But mostly, I really believe that in this world,
I wouldn't have to wonder whether I am valuable enough to be

with you.
Because it isn't about value; it's about love.
And love is something that you cannot just shove
In a corner, hoping it will come back
Once you're ready and take her back,
Hoping it will be without a crack.

Is That Love?

Is it love when I think about you when I am hopeless?
Is it love when I see you only when I can't see myself?
Is it love if I blame myself for your bad actions?
Is it love if I crave for your attention but act like I don't care?
Is it love? Or hatred? Do I miss you, or am I just lonely?
Is it love if I only love the idea of you?
Is it love if high expectations were created within our relationship?
But I'm not sure you created them
Is it love if I don't trust you but tell you all my secrets?
Is it love if I needed space from you, but then space no longer equalled freedom but control?
Is it love if I remember all of the good stuff about us
But have trouble remembering the bad things?
Is it love if it's not mutual but feels like it is?
Is it love?

Do My Looks Define Me

This square piece of glass defines my worth,
My confidence, my perspective, my whole life.
It makes me feel either big or small.
It makes me feel stupid or smart.
I wish I could just see my reflection and feel the same, but I can't.
I wish I saw beyond the skin, but I can't.
I see the book's cover and already assume its chapters.
I wish I didn't, but I do…

Tumble

You know you've fallen down when you try so hard to not let that drop fall on your face, but it does.
You know you've fallen down when you start writing poems.
You know you've fallen down when dancing doesn't make you smile.
You know you've fallen down when moving pictures don't make you forget.
You know you've fallen down when you don't see any other images other than your room for a while.
You know you've fallen down when some child's song makes you cry.
You know you've fallen down when everything seems pointless.

Every time my father sees, this death stare in my eyes,
This defeat in my body,
Laying on the bed, he asks me "Did somebody die?"
I fight the urge to not tell him that yes, someone did. It's me.
Now I know I've fallen down.

A Letter to a Dear Friend

It's ripping my heart seeing you like this,
So helpless, so tired.
I wish I could help you, when I see you break down,
But I just stare at you so intensely, following every move you make,
Produce every tear you do,
In hopes that I understand you better,
Help you feel better.
When you leave, I see nothing.
For me, you are beautiful no matter how much makeup you put on,
Although I put it on too.
I know you the most;
We dance together,
We sing together,
We cry together.
I see you when you get ready or when you take off your make up after a long day.
I see you listen to your favourite music or just spend time in silence.
When I cannot see clearly, you help me. We are best pals.
I just wish that sometimes on your worst days when your self-esteem is low,
You would still look at me with the same confidence as you do when you sing to me.
So, my twin I hope someday we will be okay.
Your dear friend, Mirror.

I Feel Like I Lost Myself

I'm not the same girl that would get excited while going to a toy shop.
I'm not the same girl that would dance around the room,
Not caring about any imperfections.
Running and screaming with disgust when a boy's name was mentioned,
I loved myself, I loved all of me.
I felt okay with who I was, with colourful pencils running around the paper,
Rather than my face.
I was happy with being alone.

Prison for My Thoughts

I wonder with my eyes around the room.
Isn't it amazing how no sense of time
can make your heart beat faster?
I look around.
Everything looks the same, but I am different.
At first, this place provided me with excitement and wonder as to what may come next.
Now, I worry as to what may come next.
I cannot say I feel lonely,
Because although I healed to the extent my body let me,
I don't want to be associated
With the objects that caused my wounds in the first place.
At the same time,
I wait for their approval, for them to like me,
Because I too feel alone but only in my mind.
Whether I'm busy in a crowded city
Or in the comfort of my bedroom,
I am able to escape from my thoughts for a while.
But why is it that I always need to run?
Why can't I reach the finish line?

Home

I want to go home.
I am in a house,
A house with walls,
With framed pictures
I recognise myself in,
A house with my belongings, my family.

But I want to go home,
The place where my childhood is hidden,
Where I feel safe,
Where I was scared of a monster under my bed,
The home that was so far away from my friends.
The home where I grew up,
Where I cried,
The home where I was constantly finding myself,
This house knows the repaired me,
The one entering a new phase,
But what I need is a home,
That knows me for who I was.

Defence

I have a weapon,
But not the kind that kills,
The kind that helps,
The kind that shields,
Me from my demons.
The kind that makes people unaware of my struggles.
I am sad, but I am happy.
I am angry, but I am happy.
I am happy, but I am happy.
Though anxiety is an armed imposter,
Damaging my inner self,
But I have a shield.
Although he lives inside, winning his wars,
He will never see the daylight behind these bars.

Metal Hearts

I am an extrovert that has to be surrounded by people,
I don't like.
I hate being in a crowd,
In the city.
Not because I'm antisocial,
But because I haven't met any "real people" yet.
I've met robots,
Fake machines with metal masks.
They play people just to hurt them,
Because they don't feel;
Their hearts are metal too.

Calendar Mark

I don't want to make money off my sadness;
Why can't it be happiness?
I want to succeed in being happy.
Not constantly breaking down and crying.
I stare at myself expecting tears to fall,
But my cheeks are dry.
Have I already run out of tears?
Am I supposed to store all my problems now?
Is that what you want me to do?
But what problems?
I don't have any.
Then why do I feel like I do?
I mark the day in the calendar;
Everything checks off.
It's time to be sad.

Memoria Damnum

I don't have any memory loss,
I don't have trouble recalling
My previous actions.
I don't give up to any distractions;
I am fully aware of my history,
And my life isn't a mystery.
Although I don't let my mind try to forget,
Try to sip an imaginary liquid,
Making me feel left
Alone at a place that doesn't feel like home.
I still sometimes wander off,
Letting my mind grow legs.
I go to the bus stop,
Hoping to escape.
My mind doesn't know what it expects,
But my legs know that they just want to go home,
Whatever home means.
They know that there will be peace.
Despite the fact that not all of us suffer from a wandering mind,
We all want to be happy,
Not only on paper.

Anguish

I am full of hope,
As I watch my little flower,
Hoping it will bloom.
Every day I add water,
I bring it sunlight.
On rainy days,
I distract my plant from the lack of energy it has.
I help her grow.
Each day, as I only see the skinny stalk
Without colourful petals,
I lose a sparkle in my eye.
How can it not bloom yet?
Is she upset?

Ghosts of the Past

You live inside my mind,
Even though I never told you to stay.
You make sure that even when I feel loved,
I walk away.
I moved on from the memories you created,
But the ghost of the lessons I learned
Never leave me waiting.
This ghost infiltrates the new people I meet,
Making me believe that it's you again I see.
I feel the breeze of fresh air on my cheeks,
I feel the stone lifting off my chest, making me at peace.
That's when you want me to believe
That I need you to breathe.
Even if I was perfectly fine on my own,
You put me on life support.
Making me believe it's you that I need,
And all that happens within the body that belongs to me.
You don't interfere with my life's choices,
But the voices you left always have me wondering.
They cast a spell on my trust,
They make me feel lost.
I am trying to escape,
But I will always have a heart with a scrape.

Leftovers

Why do I always get the leftovers?
The rubbish that no one bothers to pick up.
Placed in a location invisible to the human eye.
Why can't my love be as beautiful and exciting for me,
As it is for the person on the other end?
I stare at the sky hoping for a change,
But all I get are mere coins.
The unbearable pain in my joints,
Laying me down on this cold floor,
Making me wonder when will I ever let go?

Earth problems

Power, kingdom, ownership,
Yet no love
Since having a population to control
Is considered to be above.
Men feeling the need to carry stones
Creating not individuals but clones
The word "leader"
Mistaken for God
The word "feminism"
Mistaken for an insult
The education teaching hate and competition
Sitting in chairs that have been there since colonialism
People running around with bullets in their hands
While others struggle
To call for a ceasefire with their own heads
Men hating on women.
Women hating on men.
Society hating on immigrants.
Immigrants hating on rich
Rich hating on poor
There is no end to this "war"
Languages causing division between humanity
Forgetting the dot seen from the universe is our home
There is no segregation of where we come from
But humans still forget
What living actually means
Killing others while,
In reality killing their own hopes and dreams.

Social Battery

Why is meeting people such a chore for me?

At first, I feel like a feather drifting free,
But then I get so caught up in my thoughts,
I fall into this routine of shooting shots.
At myself, at my mind,
Convinced that all I do is cry inside.
I cannot keep smiling
When my soul feels like it's dying.
From nothing in particular,
But it feels like the mountains are collapsing,
And I'm in the middle aware of this tragedy,
But I never know how to show it.
How to own it.

At first, I crave for someone to know,
While watching people on shows.
Not wanting to be apart from each other,
Not even for a second,
Or wanting to be with each other forever.
To me, "forever" doesn't sound romantic,
It sounds like a trap set to make me frantic.
At the same time when I sit in my room,
I wonder if there is someone, I know that I will adore.
Maybe someone that doesn't say "forever,"
But simply enjoys being together,
Alone in our thoughts,
Comforting each other when they get tied in knots.
Although sometimes I feel like I meet people that don't make my social battery run out,
They usually don't want to stay for a while.

Sandcastles

I think I need to start building sand castles,
Let myself draw sand around my body,
Taking turns to get more water, yelling, "I'm ready!"
Ready for an adventure, a snippet of creativity,
Letting myself get absorbed by this activity.
A single strand of hair drifts into my view,
Using my hands to brush it away.
Focusing on the castle alone,
Traveling to the world of magic and hope.
Then carrying the sand everywhere I go,
Being frustrated why is it still with me?
Even though I left the castle on the beach.

Now I just sit at the beach,
Watching how other kids follow their dreams.
Making sand castles,
While I make sure that my hair
stays the same as before.
Even though,
I didn't care enough to not let my inner child let go.

Sun

Visage

I love how there are so much faces in the world,

Each one has their own name,
Each one has their own time for fame.
Each has a story to play,
A history to say.

Without these faces,
The world wouldn't be complete.
For some, a face may not trigger any feelings,
But for others, the sight of "the face",
may stop them from healing.
For others, "the face" could be considered a work of art,
Yet, for that person, their face is what makes them fall apart.

Each one of us is going in the same direction,
But sometimes choosing different roads.
Those roads may break at different junctures,
Building a person's character,
As they transform into a forager.
Those faces may react differently to different surroundings,
Some might feel they've spent their whole life as a foundling.
Some might experience different pains,
But after all, we are all the same.
Going in the same direction.
Hoping for a guide to follow,
But for now we all wallow.
For our obstacles, for our goals,
Filling out these empty holes,
In our self-esteem.
Projecting the life on the screens,
Wishing it wasn't only in our dreams.

Somnia
(Dreams)

Sometimes I like to hide,
I like to hide in dreams.
In dreams where the only inch of reality is that I am in them.
In dreams that are full of creativity,
Magic and love.
Dreams are the dimension that we all aspire to achieve.
Dreams help me move forward;
In dreams, my soul is free.
My mind is calm,
There is no storm.

Dreams are where people don't rush,
Where they aspire to live,
Rather than prove a point,
That isn't meant to be proven.
Where there is no illusion.
All the places in dreams feel like a warm embrace.

The air is fresh,
With every breath.
Your lungs are full without any pain,
As you dance in the rain.
droplets glide off your skin,
So delicate.
The skin feels so vellicate.
Someday dreams will become my reality,
But for now, I will stick to the actuality.

Volets Bleus
(Blue Shutters)

I look ahead of me,
The mosaic of shining circles dangling on a small rope,
The people with painted hope.
Windows with greenery covering their faces,
Scraped paint, happy faces.
With colourful drapes,
In motion caused by the delicate wind;
If not for the curtains waving,
The people wouldn't be embracing.
Its contribution,
So focused on the town's beauty,
The nature's duty.
The rumble in the village,
So pleasing to the ear;
Here, there is no fear,
Of disappointment,
Just pure enjoyment.
The streets getting more narrow,
Comforting you with touch,
When life isn't helping you much.
Mixture of bricks
Forming a building,
Filled with history,
Greeting with the old signs of mystery.
Slowly forming a line of people,
Waiting so cheerful.
Guided by the smell from small cafes,
Looking at the sky forming different shapes.
With the help of the sun and clouds,
You can easily get absorbed by these warm crowds.

Time

People say time is precious,
I agree.
But not because it goes quickly,
And by the time you notice, you leave.
I agree because with time my wounds heal.
With time, I can be free.
With time, old friends come around.
With time, I cannot hear these annoying sounds,
Reminding me of my loneliness.
Of my tardiness,
Of the mistakes I've made.
Although time can sometimes make you wait,
You have a feeling that it's late,
You might forget it for a while,
And feel like you can just cry.
You stop appreciating the time now,
Because the time later will heal you,
The time now is the process.
A process so important but so invisible, you might forget it
Time can reveal itself to you in different forms:
Your appearance,
Your smile's interference,
Your mindset changing,
Or your tears fading.
Although time still runs,
Leaving new scars,
You know now that it won't stop,
And will rescue you eventually,
And make you feel on top.
So although time can sometimes make you wait,
Remember,
With time, everything becomes ok.

Spectrum of Love

Love is a concept,
That I so desperately needed in my life.
I felt that my happiness,
Wouldn't bloom if I didn't have someone to hold.
Now I understand that love is a spectrum,
Shown in different forms.
And although I don't have someone to hold,
My body is filled with love,
No other person can show.

The love from within,
The synonym of embracing,
Believing in yourself and what you're facing.
Not needing the validation from others,
But simply enjoying the moment.
Not craving another component.

There come days when I feel empty inside,
Hoping someone would fill that hole in my life.
Now I know that isn't loneliness;
It's my body recharging from hopelessness.
From the challenges in the past,
From the battles that had to be fought fast.
And once I feel free again,
The love comes back from within,
Telling me, I can.